D0125630

Pebble™

Wetland Animals

Beavers

by Margaret Hall

Consulting Editor: Gail Saunders-Smith, Ph.D.
Consultant: Charlie Luthin, Executive Director
Wisconsin Wetlands Association, Madison, Wisconsin

Capstone
press

Mankato, Minnesota

Pebble Books are published by Capstone Press
151 Good Counsel Drive, P.O. Box 669, Mankato, Minnesota 56002
http://www.capstonepress.com

1 2 3 4 5 6 09 08 07 06 05 04

Library of Congress Cataloging-in-Publication Data
Hall, Margaret, 1947–
    Beavers/by Margaret Hall.
    p. cm.—(Wetland animals)
    Summary: Photographs and simple text introduce the characteristics and
behavior of beavers.
    Includes bibliographical references and index.
    ISBN 0-7368-2063-9 (hardcover)
    1. Beavers—Juvenile literature. [1. Beavers.] I. Title. II. Series.
QL737.R632 H36 2004
599.37—dc21   2003008552

Note to Parents and Teachers

The Wetland Animals series supports national science standards
related to life science. This book describes and illustrates beavers.
The photographs support early readers in understanding the
text. The repetition of words and phrases helps early readers
learn new words. This book also introduces early readers to
subject-specific vocabulary words, which are defined in the
Glossary section. Early readers may need assistance to read some
words and to use the Table of Contents, Glossary, Read More,
Internet Sites, and Index/Word List sections of the book.

Table of Contents

Beavers

Beavers are rodents
with large front teeth.
Rodents are mammals.

Beavers have brown fur and webbed feet.
They have flat tails.

places where beavers live

8

Wetlands

Beavers live in wetlands
in North America
and Europe. Wetlands are
areas of land covered by
water and plants.

9

What Beavers Do

Beavers swim and dive under the water.

Beavers slap their tails
on the water. The sound
warns other beavers
of danger.

Beavers cut tree trunks
and branches with
their sharp teeth.
They eat the bark.

16

Beavers build dams
from branches and mud.
Ponds form near dams.

Beavers build homes called lodges. Beavers use sticks, plants, and mud to make the lodges.

Day and Night

Beavers sleep in lodges during the day. They go out at dusk to eat. Beavers work all night.

Glossary

dam—a wall that stops water from flowing in a stream or river

dusk—the time of day after sunset when it is almost dark

lodge—a rounded home made of sticks, plants, and mud; a lodge has an underwater door.

mammal—a warm-blooded animal with a backbone; female mammals feed milk to their young.

rodent—a mammal with large, sharp front teeth; beavers, mice, rats, and squirrels are rodents.

webbed—having folded skin or tissue between an animal's toes or fingers; beavers use their webbed feet to swim.

wetland—an area of land covered by water and plants; marshes, swamps, and bogs are wetlands.

Read More

Donovan, Sandra. *A Beaver in Its Lodge.* Where Do Animals Live? Minneapolis: Lake Street Publishers, 2003.

Galko, Francine. *Wetland Animals.* Animals in Their Habitats. Chicago: Heinemann Library, 2003.

Turner, Matt. *Beavers.* The Secret World Of. Chicago: Raintree, 2004.

Internet Sites

FactHound offers a safe, fun way to find Internet sites related to this book. All of the sites on FactHound have been researched by our staff.

Here's how:

1. Visit *www.facthound.com*

2. Type in this special code **0736820639** for age-appropriate sites. Or enter a search word related to this book for a more general search.

3. Click on the Fetch It button.

FactHound will fetch the best sites for you!

Index/Word List

Word Count: 119
Early-Intervention Level: 13

Editorial Credits
Sarah L. Schuette, editor; Patrick Dentinger, series designer; Scott Thoms, photo researcher; Karen Risch, product planning editor

Photo Credits
Bruce Coleman Inc./Lee Foster, 16; Norman Tomalin, 6
Corbis, 4, 8
Heather R. Davidson, 1
Superstock, cover
Tom & Pat Leeson, 12, 14
Tom Stack & Associates/Brian Parker, 20; Thomas Kitchin, 10, 18